EPIGRAMS

OF

INFINITY

EPIGRAMS
OF
INFINITY

JAMES KARIS

AVALINI

Epigrams of Infinity
Copyright © 2018 by James Karis

ISBN: 978-0-9715270-6-5

First Edition
ABCDEFGHIJK

Published by
AVALINI
1343 Main Street
Fitchburg, MA 01420

Editors: Clare Karis, Rand Refrigeri, Ruth Berube
Cover painting and back cover photo by James Karis

For more information about us, please contact AVALINI, 1343 Main Street, Fitchburg, MA 01420 or visit us at www.avalini.com.

INFINITY

Reflection of a wren
  shatters kitchen light.

It may be seen
  from one perspective,
    a thousand perspectives,

infinite perspectives.

The bird does not fly because he has wings.

One light—
  neither created
    nor extinguished.

        Mirror shatters sun

in the wren of reflection.

The bird flies
because he is dreaming.

PENDULUM

Memory of snow

        falls into the mind.

               Angels converse

      in cherub tongue.

Conjoined glow

        of invisible candles,

the scent of mist,

as an empty tree swing

    weaves

                  between

      pendulous

                        snowflakes

and slowly rocks into stillness

               and dark.

THE FINAL EMBER

Each moment passing—

the final ember
of a dying fire.

When was it
that I ceased to be
                a little boy?

Like the last sliver
        of the setting sun ...

            and sooner than you think,

it is gone.

CATERPILLAR

Train pulls out
of the station.

Electric orchids race
past waxen clouds,

river,
warehouse,

beyond Gandhi graffiti
in red and rhapsody.

Ambiguity rises from water—

September folds
into birch trees.

I meditate in spray paint
on wet brick.

INDIGO SLEEP

Summer wind
　　and late linen curtains—

midday enters the room,
　　　sparingly, in spidery shadows

refracted by triangular
panes of indigo glass,

　　　　through the silent day
　　　　　　that strums the slats

of an oak chair
into a warm melody

　　　　of shadow and calm.

UNRIPPLED

Taper star,
allow rain rest.

Droplets fall into puddle,
rippling reflected stars.

A single cloud above puddle,
beside star.

Stars are unrippled,
and yet, rippled.

The cloud moves away.

Unity within multiplicity.

Rain tapers,
allowing stars to rest.

The away moves cloud.

Rest, star—
allow taper rain.

TONGUE

She pours me a sip of Pinot Noir
from her amethyst lips.

Our tongues dance,
mingling in liquid silk.

There is nothing to do
but taste the wine.

My eyes are Tongue,
my ears—Tongue,
my being—Tongue.

I am Tongue and eternity,
Tongue and perpetual shape,
Tongue and liquiform.

I am Tongue and she is Taste,
naked in the original garden, unashamed.

I am content to be nothing but Tongue,
unlimited in the gamut of the grape,
entangled in the rapturous vine.

I am Tongue and I am deathless.
I am Tongue—immortal.

THE INVISIBLE

November—
                  the oak grows into
   its nakedness.

Rising sun greets shade
        on fervent snow.

Naked oak becomes oak chair.

Frozen pond
            is written
in the language of ice skates.

The most indelible of all things
has never been marked.

That which has never been marked
       may never be erased.

THE INFINITE WOOD

In the back yard—
      raking, piling leaves
      into tall brown bags.

       The last of the setting sun

on tired shoulders.

A sip of cold beer.
A glance at the infinite wood.

There is no point in rushing.

       More leaves will soon fall.

FIVE FISHNET STOCKINGS

Four black

and one white.

Hanging from a frayed clothesline,

five fishnet stockings

fastened with wooden pins.

Wind blows hemlock

in eleven o'clock limelight.

I don't know if the stocking fell

or if it never existed.

ILLUMINATION

In the garden of fire,
the sunflower cannot be found.

Not that it isn't there.

Cherokee chief in sunflower field;

trees are calm

in green evening.

Sun speaks to him
in tentacles of light.

Petals of sun
are day—their eyes,

the face of night.

New Cold Space

No one wants to talk to clouds,
not even oranges.
But the cheese drawer
still needs to be emptied.
The new one comes tomorrow
and I have to part with
various jams and marmalades
that've been opened once
and never again
and left there for years
to grow different colored molds.
It's a cleansing experience.
It makes you decide
what's worth keeping and what isn't.
I think I'll keep the mustard—
just opened that
and it's spicy brown
which I like with pastrami.
But I think that dried orange
way in the back
near last year's yogurt
is going in the trash

even though it has sentimental value.

I feel cleaner already,

the space around me,

and now I don't need to think

about mold spores affecting my fruit.

The new one comes tomorrow

and it'll be strange for a while

but I'll get through,

and I'll make sure I have a place

for fresh fruit and pastrami

next to the spicy brown

and maybe some fresh yogurt.

I feel calmer now, and cleaner.

The clouds have opened

and a flash of orange hits the room.

The new one comes tomorrow

so I'll dust the empty space

to be sure it feels welcome.

It'll be good, I think.

I can't wait for new cold space.

It'll be good, I think.

I can't wait.

Upon Waking

First car to pass
        with the new day.

                A momentary slashing
through the wind of Semillon dawn.

Perhaps not even a car,
        but a ghost of the diligent street,
seeking a place to rest

              amid endless miles

and infinite intersections of time.

Always tired but always awake,
    curiously meandering into the white.
        Grounded but hovering, not expecting.

Always a blank road, firmly retraced.

And the light of day was new

              and
    carefully

                  scattered.

BREAKFAST

Rectangles frame wicker.

Twilight draped by autumn wood,

melting frost on amaryllis tepals.

Earth is painted air

in a dark room.

Morning bathes parquet.

There is symmetry

in falling shadows.

As I Look Back at Her

I see her
       across a dream
in a crowded room.

A child finds
       an old man
   in the mirror.

I don't know
  what the wind
   is whispering this night

to the steeped-in-summer pine.

The only path
     out of the labyrinth

is through yourself.

THE HORNET

He plants tomatoes
    in hymeneal earth
        as a hornet circles his ear.

        He almost feels one with it,
    even though he can't fly
  and can't imagine
the sensation of weightlessness.

Soil buries itself
    under his fingernails
        which is calming and good.

      Rain smells of grass,
drastic, bold in the day.

Gardenias watch him
    as he kneels and digs.

He envies the hornet,
but his admiration is stronger.

THE TIDE

Raindrops dot the bay

        and ripple the mind.

A wooden dock,

beiged by the paint of time.

They hold hands,

walking the beach in twilight.

Rain clouds veil

        the sky,

reducing and yet multiplying its glow

above ashen seaweed.

Lenient sun

evenings the world to sleep

as footprints on the shore

        write a love story

forgotten by the tide.

How She Feels About Lemons

Her black coat,

serrated paint in sunlight,

the only ray of redemption

beaming through

the desperate alcoves

of her eyes.

The air, shimmering cobalt

through her dirty hair,

her bruised fingertips

that match the night.

Mojito

Lawn on sun
reflects window.

Wind blows mint plants
and I say hello to them.

Night comes until
remain sky gray
to pass the sing cloud
to wait
birds pass.

Clear sky reflecting lake still,

clear sky and bird song.

BEFORE THE FUNERAL

Blackness blankets field
of maple
burning morning sun.

Wind with sympathy
in yellow shadow motionless.

Finally camouflaged
is maple tree,
candied stardust
trance night whisper.

To pass through life
like a dark thought
through frozen treetops.

A little girl pours maple syrup
over pancakes
as morning clouds sunbathe,
ambling toward eternity.

BOYHOOD

The mossy velvet patch

    at the base

        of an oak.

I imagine being

inside

        the tree

and there is no separation,

the fusion

    of space and mind.

Deep beneath

        the twiggy

    oregano stems

        from last year

lurk honey-emerald leaves.

I wonder if

    they loitered there

    through the winter

or if they are new,

          now,

with the mud

and disjointed shrieks

of children in the evening street.

I grow for two hundred years

  and finally

a boy runs his fingers

across my velvet moss.

GRATITUDE

Red wine eyes
sepia the sky—
        lilacs lost
below lullaby plumage.

Trees of the moon
accept not the dawn
but for its blind embrace.

As I light my pipe
in my creaky cradle,
first smoke ascends
from autumn's chimney.

I exhale a plume
of purple mist
        as pine trees
wave dangerously
at the maître d' of dusk.

Roller coasters

                    and sunrises

are blinks of my eyes
and tattered pages
of my dreams.

Rusty watering pail
reflected in rainwater,
a strobe of lightning.

I sit at the kitchen table
as she sleeps above.

Happiness is the instant
before you know you are happy.

CAUSALITY

Clouds have come
to find crickets.

The bottle on the table
and the lantern that illuminates the bottle.

The sound of the door
slamming across the street.

Fog meets lavender evening.

Your next sip of wine already exists
in perfect siphood.

If it didn't,
there would be no slamming door.

AWAKENED AT A TRAIN STOP

We are riders

    on a wave

        of timeless light—

radiant beings, immortal,

slowed for but an instant

to glimpse the frozen frame of time.

I stand beyond midnight

in wet newborn grass

and look to the stars.

Train pulls forth

from the station

and all is once again

          a blur.

CATERPILLAR AFTER RAIN

Poppies close their eyes
and harmonize with night.

How strange
that only darkness
enables us to see the stars.

Fade evening,
commune raven.

He dissolves into day
as time rises
in the east.

Butterflies incinerated by rainbows.

WHERE SHE TOUCHES HERSELF

She runs to the barn

      when the noise is too much,

            when she needs solvency

and the sound of hay.

She looks up to the window

            and studies nightfall,

      how it fills the room

with undulating trellises of beige

and yawning shadows

          of smoke-painted day.

GRANDMOTHER

Stars incubate infinity.

Afternoon is cloud
until clear come.

At the center
of a starlit forest
in a dream,
candle swan eye dance.

On the surface of water
also rests the surface of space.

Dagger scent of winter
replaces naked skin.

Swan dance star eye see.

Muted white by snowflake pattern
sun diagonal
        warmth clear.

Young grass
tinsel light reflect
mirror blizzard moon.

CONTRAST

A machine angrily hums

           in the park

as a woman

        in smooth broken glass

             walks her family of sheep.

Sitting on a bench,

           savoring a cold breath

              of forest air,

an old man wonders
where life has gone

         and why he sits alone.

SHADOW RIPPLES, UNION

Saxophone moans

         in fetal bathlight.

    Her breasts

        frame water

           in shadow ripples.

A drop from her nipple

enters the tub,

       never to be seen

               again.

CONCEPTION

Vacant boundary
>   of liquid puzzles

blends with the universe,
>   endless edge—

>   consciousness
>>   displaced into
>   the perception of fire.

Imagine yourself
>   by looking at the dark light
on the absence of symmetry.

LABRADOR AND DRAGONFLY

Black Labrador
        extends his tongue
                toward morning's puddle.

Listening hovers beside dragonfly.

                Tongue scoops water

              or water catches tongue?

                        Lapping—the only sound.

Shadows grab summer syntaxes
and treetops are retraced.

Thirst now quenched,

                the puddle stills

                    and resumes reflecting.

Hospital, December

Twilight intersects
with blossoming stars
as moon kisses dusk.

Ocher wind fills infinity
with falling leaves
and skies are water fields
of late autumn ambrosia.

Forests become brushstrokes
erased in harmonious invisibilities.

Sky is rippled
by stones skimmed across
the division of day and night
by winter's children.

Although clouds part
beyond ambivalent shadows
of fading rain,
I think of waiting in line
for starlit frost
as a way of growing old.

FATHER

I see the sapling
and watch myself being born.

A cloud passes the sun
as a daydream trances the land.

I watch as the final leaf
falls from the elm.

A painted river
to the other side
of the earth,
both child and mother.

I am her father and child.

Staircase in the trees,
doorway guarded
by a purple-spotted iguana.

My face is cold.

BROKEN DAWN

The empty cup
contains itself
and so it is full.

Torn sunrise
into fragments of rain
diminishes.

White cloud long with sky.

Rooibos tea boils
in response
to evening insight.

Rusty bridge
across today
for the first time.

Ignorance met with pain
is the creator of understanding.

MONKEY TO MAN

In the jungle of amaranth,
vagaries of beige
rise in emerald.

If you look into my eyes
you will see two moons.

Moon only one
although eyes see two.

The monkey eats leaves
but prefers figs.

LEMON CELLOS

A million painted Amalfian ladies
dance in the sky

above Ferris wheel streets

illuminated by the reflection
of star-speckled puddles.

Overflowing flutes of sparkling
lemon cellos play a sunny tune

as lemon light
bathes yellow sand

in gradient luminous intensities.

BIRTH

First bird morning song,
meaning from darkness.

Splotches of white and doubt
play upon stained glass
in burning wind.

Duality is the root of delusion.

Treetops paint pale
silver courtyard
with
        declining
                lavender
                        sun.

Stone steps extend
cool welcome

                of evening.

NONCONFORMITY

The heart of the elk
is to be neither fathomed
nor diminished.

To stand alone, anonymously,
both persistent

                     and transformed,
unfathomed and undiminished,

intervals of darkness
elevated into the night,
reaching above
              the dawn,
against the gray,
the rain,

      the scatter of time.

WOMB

Moon relaxed

       by frost-covered glass.

She climbs the stairs,
       into her room,

drops her robe,

into bed,

       nude, in January.

Morning comes
as she sleeps.

       Frost calms.

Window through sun,

       disrobed.

LIMBO

Is it I sitting here
                on this old green bench,
talking to a cloud
and feeding the ducks
in a gray glow
                as rain begins
to speckle the pond
with timeless momentary craters?

Am I only her breath,
                her eyes, the myriad sleep,
        dreaming myself into
the cradle of her voice,
the cloud above—

                the ceaseless rain?

WHISKERS

They weren't there this morning,
                 after he shaved,
or as he made his coffee
and waited for the dawn.

My grandfather
          smoking his pipe
                  on the front steps
after dinner,

hot night
          that smells of sumac,

the way the day
          dims for the stars,

church bell chiming
          in the distance

                       as the moon arrives.

They weren't there this morning,

       after he shaved,

but now they are,

                silvery,

      jagged,

gleaming in moonlight
as he puffs his pipe

and watches the night

          in the trees.

JEANS BELOW BLACK CLOUDS AT SUNSET

Personality of raindrops
transformed by blooming
citrus celestial streaks
slowing weary wind
in the auditorium of morning
yawning the rain to sleep
beyond splotches of certainty
beneath overcast denim smudges
of slowing drowsy night
into the eyes and ears
and fragmented conversations
of hallucinating blackbirds.

THE BLUE, STATICKY 3 A.M.

She threw her arms
behind her head as if to say,
"I am free—I am yours."

I drank her,
drank her peachy jazz sweet,
drank her until
I was thirsty again.

We fell asleep
in a sonic cocoon
of off-white echoes,
candles and rain.

She was a glossy new photo,
smooth and viscous, like blood,

but dry,

with her left leg
draped inwardly,
asleep in bed
in the blue, staticky 3 a.m.

BORN IN THE WIND

The only reason
       I come to this place
is to feel
    the overlapping shadows
       of winter
while I smell frost
             being   born
listening
    to the reflection
      of my face
        in the pond
as it rattles
               in the wind.

FLAMENCO

Moon seduces orange grove
   to the sounds
      of a sedated guitar.

Sky divides mountain
   with raindrops
      of a million years.

The scent of oranges
   before hot rain.

Fingers that strum a guitar
after silence, before silence.

Nature creates mountain.

*Nature creates river
flow through mountain.*

*Nature destroys
mountain.*

Nature creates canyon.

Moon blinks a snapshot
   of an orange grove.

INVINCIBLE

How fitful the fantasy
　of a train
wending through serpents of mist,
　　rising through naked trees
as shadows dance
　between clouds copulating
with sleeping crystal ponds.

A chimney puffs
a smoke ring
through a smoke ring.

Only this time of fall,
alive with leaves of envy,
　　is my driveway sad.

How invincible, the train—
that it may witness

　　　　and then pass along.

CHOPPING ROSEMARY

Dissolve sunset
swim across
untamable forest.

Bootless children climb

       immeasurable mountains

     through muddy snow

     in the imagination

 of rain clouds.

Behind cobblestones,
                an axe splinters wood.

The scent of pine
                      is discovered.

An ant climbs the fence
and then descends.

He told me to enjoy my coffee.

MONA

My most vivid memories of her

are when she was clothed

and I was naked,

because I was vulnerable, wild—

a blue aborigine

in the burning bedroom,

no separation

from the rapturous One,

blending unfettered

into a newborn universe,

unhidden from her eyes

or from infinity.

WABI-SABI

White curtain
behind morning
peers the sun.

A tilted fence
in snow
straightened by time.

I blink—
and find the red evening
                 of July.

Into day, darkness
fades into wood.

Have you ever watched icicles
sculpted by the wind?

FREE

All is transient, save the mind.

Bumblebee
    above red sedum

           above the grave.

Eternity is a link of consciousness.

Diamond sun
warms headstone
in diamond mind.

As long as consciousness exists,
we are all immortal.

She flies away,
the woman's soul—

unencumbered,

          with wings.

THE SCREEN

I went to the movies
to watch the screen,
not the images on the screen,
but the screen itself,
blank and white,
perfect in its simplicity,
empty and capable
of containing anything.
Then the pictures started,
the noise began,
loud noises and bright moving pictures
replacing all of that divine white.
People stopped talking
as if something had started,
but for me it had ended.
So I left,
renewed and clarified,
filled with potential again,
as I reentered a world
of loud noises
and bright moving pictures
better able to cope with them,
to see the screen
behind their tempting illusion,
only the screen,
white and clear,
always there,
empty
and containing everything.

THE BRIDGE

She is the bridge for humanity
across the vast unknown,
into the jungle of light.

They cross, one by one,
awakened in the full moon's garden.

But when the last one has crossed
and she longs to join them,

where is   her bridge?

HONESTY

On a wet glass tabletop,
        raindrops crash
           into the reflection
of birch trees.

A rusty shed
rises above morning mist.

Daybreak is green
        and nature's awakening
     vanishes in the shadow
of picnic umbrellas.

The truth requires more craft
than does deception.

The Artwork of Impermanence

Styrofoam coffee cup
hopscotches down
the spectral street
as the impetuous sky
erases wingstrokes of owls.

Clouds part
        for the lips of lovers
        naked in a doorway.

How ingenious,
the singular hand of time
        on the canvas of empty space.

Sun sets
    on chimney
atop a slate roof
like Aeolian harps
    into infinity.

How incredible are the trees
that wave in the wind
on an earnest eve

or butterflies making love
        on a tulip?

MINDFUL

The gentle tapping
of sleet on the windowpane

is all there is

as the hands of autumn
revolve.

There is no I
and no thinking

                    no hearing

only the windowpane rattling

                    as winter falls.

THESE...

Crescent moon rises
   between two trees,
    pine and elm.

Behind the first,
   silver cloud.

Behind the second,
   first star of night.

Clarity meets obscurity.

These trees
  that watch children at play
 in fallen leaves.

These evenings that recede
   into winter's white eyes.

These branches
  that become one
 with the sky
  as fallen shadows.

A beetle circles
an apple, endlessly,
thinking he's getting somewhere.

HER WARMTH

She was asleep
in oily, blackberry
iridescence—vibrant.

Until she moved relaxedly
with a slight, mindless breath.

She stirred and awoke.

Like a rare flower
that rises at dawn
and lasts for but a moment,
blossoming its perfection
upon a faulted world.

INDIVISIBLE

                        Mirror on pond,
unsettled by rain.

        Until it is no more—
                        dawn meadow,
night unseen.

When you find your center,

                you will have found its limit.

Sky is scuffed

                by orange glass,

but it has not died
                in the mist of weeping.

    Dawn night,
unseen meadow.

Lightning flashes
                                past eyes
        of a hillside.

The edge of the universe

                is the center of the mind.

INSIGHT

He entered paradise
a blind man
in a land of light.

He couldn't see his wife,
but his soul communed
with hers
like moonbeams intertwined.

He searched his darkness
for a single point of light
and he found it on a warm day
as he listened to his children's laughter,

lost in play.

SUBLIMINAL

An ambient flurry
begins its dance.

But it won't be cause
for shovels to scrape sidewalks.

A snowflake
    ambles downward
and melts as soon
as it greets
      warm spring earth.

Once it meets the ground,
it is only a drop of water,
indistinguishable from all the rest.

The astral dance of the snowflake,
now—but now, not here,
Vivaldi playing
in the next room,
quiet and abating,

to listen, something to watch,
no cause for concern
with its drifting dance
embracing the house.

Now it is here.

Dark tree skeletons
frame cloud refractions
of flaming white.

The mystery that holds
        the painting
lies in the brush
that holds the mystery.

How short,
the lifespan of the snowflake.

How fleeting, the art
        of nature.

MOTHER

I pick blueberries
  from a bush
    deep in my memory.
Twilight—a field,
  the peppery scent
              of blueberries
        in the solemn sun.
She—painted by the rising moon,
  fingerprints
          flapping in the wind.
Blueberries, tobacco
      and late summer
          inside a blueberry patch
          as the sun sets on childhood.
I wonder if yesterday
has finally come
as I look upon the steam
            rising from the blueberry pie
      she made, and suddenly,
            the piece upon my plate,
the way the ice cream melts and turns blue.

The air smells
faintly of wine
which I won't understand
                    for years.

THE MONK

Last butterfly
of summer.

It takes a lifetime
            never to find

redemption.

A black and white cat dreams beside
a table of vernal basil.

Church bricks
are slightly dimmer
than yesterday.

Sun pours in
through the window

            like a June bug.

We are ova
on the river of reality.

SPACES

In the naked tree,
a raven sits and wonders,

is falling snow

                in darkness

black or white?

Copper morning glow

                deepens through grays
    of dawn rain,

        tangled in spider webs
      and bicycle spokes
    speckled with starry dew
splashed within spaces

      between porch steps.

Night silence is lifted
    by imagining constellations sideways.

NAVEL

Rain cloud drinks the serpent.

Her eyes meet
her eyes
meeting her eyes.

She kisses her way
down her neck
to her abdomen.

Serpent crosses desert,
watched by the unraining cloud.

Salty-sweet nectar
from the navel
of the goddess.

Serpent enters rain cloud.

From the lips
of one goddess
to another's navel.

From the navel
of a goddess
to the lips of the universe.

FLY

I sit in my yard
in springtide dusk
and watch a dragonfly.

"Be, fly, play,"

                 he tells me,
as he weaves figure eights
through the low sky.

"All is air," says he.

Just watch the dragon

                Fly.

SERENITY

Become simply form
because of rain.

Snow footprinted
by rain melted,
dissipating like it was young.

As slowly as the room seeps
into morning,
sun lifted.

Nothing missing and nothing needed,
how to form, but simply becoming,
because of rain
                           and eyes to see it.

Snowdrifts push footprints
into wind.

OPEN MIND

Cobblestones peek through
                holes in elderly tar.

People passing on the street
fail to notice
because they all live
in the next moment.

Cerebral triangles
trap persimmon butterflies
within spiraling chasms
of tired oak trees.

A caterpillar climbs the leg
of a rusty lawn chair

slowly

                and without intention.

GRANDFATHER

When he was alive,
I thought
my grandfather
didn't talk enough.

As I sat with him,
he was often lost in thought,
silent,
a sharp thread on his red wool sweater
occasionally teetering
with his breath.

I wanted to know
what he knew.

I wanted to see
through old eyes
while I was still young.

I now realize
          his silence

was wisdom.

REBIRTH

Ice-frosted
    sunrise windowpane:
tangerine gelato.

Hot shower
    on half-asleep skin,
steam fills the room
      and catches polygons
    of amber,
conjuring parallel realms
of cosmic humidity.

Snow still dwells
beneath the shade
      of the hedge,
but even it recedes each day
as the sun reaches evening now.

My bedroom fills
    candlelight
      perfectly,
so far away.

Why this moment,
this instant?

Orange through the horizon of oak
as a yellow pickup truck
            draws circles
in an empty parking lot.

Diamond shadows on porch wall,
peace and continuity.

For the first time
in three months
I can actually see my lawn.

New sky is clear once more
and a cool breath invigorates
with the scent
                        of mud and bloom.

WINTER DREAM OF A CAMPFIRE

Being born in moonlit wind,
my mind rests upon
the dialogue of sunset
in hydrangea.

Winter skin
                is the earth
of summer fire.

Blue stones
escape emptiness
in rising poppy blossoms.

Evergreen branches
greet each other
as cloud scorpions
        gild the sky.

The mystery of light
is a circle of stone.

Paint that chips
from the side of a fire hydrant
                is in no hurry
to complete its slow sonata
into the wilderness of time.

BALANCE

The genius of the tree
is that it progresses
             without moving.

It begins with a plan,
but lives each day
without planning.

Born with an idea,
it follows its path
with no idea.

It is present, past and future.

Rooted in the ground,
             it plays

                  in the wind.

Kokopelli

The painter's paints
are blindness and invisibility.

Porch glow through kitchen
into twilight.

Day descends
and night repels
as a lizard dances
to the melody of a flute.

In darkness,
all is the same.

> *Shadow reveals.*

And all became one,

      again,

in darkness.

> *Shadow finding.*

Evergreen hush
blankets sleeping mint
with summertime's
restless signal.

                  A dark room
illuminated by
the sad monotony
of lovemaking crickets.

Of Red Ravens

They were yellow,
orange, really,
the kind of orange
you have to look
closely at to see.
She left yesterday,
forever I think,
but I'm okay now.
They're here with me,
yellow and orange,
slowly changing,
keeping me warm
even though the days
are getting shorter
and my mind is
beginning to dwindle
like the orange sun
as day turns to evening,
orange to red,
and the ravens
perch high in the elm tree,

chattering in the cold

as if they don't care

who hears them.

Soon they will all

be red

and I will sleep

long and dark into morning,

dreaming of her,

forever I think,

of yellow and orange

and of red ravens.

BOARDWALK

Suntan oil,
somewhere in memory.

Sand dries
on the small of her back.

With each thought,
we blossom
into a new self.

Sun sets
by the breath of clouds
and she mourns
the loss of rain.

My mind drives through
an ice cream truck
at the bottom
of the ocean.

BE

As human beings,
we need concepts
to understand being.

And yet,
we consider ourselves
greater than the humble bee.

The bee does not need concepts
to understand being.

He simply bes.

PERSPECTIVE

Raising arms—
great evening breeze,
           howling moon.

Rain clouds
hide stars
as twilight kisses earth.

Moon crawls
           over declining slate;
April muddies cold air.

Spring breeze
           becomes summer wind
as lilacs bloom.

I watch darkness
lift stars
beyond the violet steeple.

You blink your eyes

and fall

                       has come.

Dancing leaves

                         impale the night

and the water of sound
rushes past
the red river.

SNOWFLAKES

It was as if the earth
blew upward,
enticing them to dance
back toward the clouds
for but an instant

then

down

again

to the last of autumn's grass,
which they coated
with delirious gestures,

crystalline sages
lost in time.

TRANSCENDENCE

On the eve of his death,

the old man was asked by his son,

"What is the essence of life?"

The old man replied:

"When you are conceived,

you transcend duality.

When you are born,

you transcend the womb.

When you create,

you transcend the beast.

When you learn,

you transcend ignorance.

When you teach,

you transcend death.

When you love,

you transcend the self."

As the sun rose,

the old man died in his sleep,

transcending pain and rejoining the universe.

DECEPTION

Rain firefly is dusk.

Descend spider clothesline.

In the web,
there is no upside down.

Warm summer
of rain,
begin.

A spider web
    will catch a strange moth
        but not a strange spider.

PRIORITY

The sounds of morning begin—
first the cars,
then the buses,
then the city trucks.

So many people
heading in so many directions
instead of one direction.

So many priorities
instead of a single priority.

The people turn
in many directions—
the earth,
     only one.

CHASM

Scorpion
    circles
        cactus,

searching for a lover.

Elephants dance
    upon their dry floor
and dress the night
with mystic dust.

Across the earth,
birch trees
    rise into morning
  like ancient tusks.

Green grass
    yearns for cacti vision.

Into day fades the final star.

Sunset early in jungle come.

SIMPLY WATCHING HER

She was mauve and curvature,
coiled in the dark bed.

She bent the morning glow
with her hips,
naked and flush with wet light,
dressed in the hue of dawn,
greens and blues
swirling into each other,
oily lusters on the medium of sleeping skin.

The light could touch her and so could I,
but my pleasure was in simply watching her,

Still

and episodic.

MARACA

Why do my eyes seem so far away?

Raising the giant oak
in my hand—a maraca
rattling in shimmering night—
my soul sings a lullaby of lust.

Meanderings of shadow
and ponderings of rain
are the only stern marks
against an absent horizon.

I dare the springness of the tree
to behold the face of aspirin winter
as a weeping wreath crowns the sky.

Through a doorway,
I am greeted by a coyote
playing a ukulele
while sparrows nest
in newborn silence
with autumn straw.

Talking to myself
about the circularity
of spray-painted caterpillars,
I watch the sky in treetops
where new buds
are quenched by my eyes.

Sun pours itself
through a colander of clouds
as branches stand apart from evening—
the sound of a rainstorm
being born in a cistern.

A hole in the sky opens
and litters the dusk
with daffodil pastels.

When the universe is my wings,
where can I fly?

THE SEEDS

On the left,
a man's grave
that is dry and barren—
unvisited, unattended.

On the right,
another man's grave,
blossoming and verdant—
a site commonly sought
for reflection and illumination.

They are graves
of the same earth,
but not of the same deeds.

Death is the garden
of the seeds we sow in life.

ENLIGHTENMENT ...

... is faster than light.

Behind a tree,
into the wood—*vanished.*

His flashings are silenced
by uninterrupted
intervals of darkness,
           clothesline-calm air,
the hum of trees,

germinating into a womb of smoke.

Not vanished in imagination.

Calm focus, loss of self ... unity.

The interval between
the flashings of a firefly
           is limitless—

like summer night,
      warm air,

         the humming of wood.

CAMPING

Lake at midnight,
persisting into reflection.

Trees made from clouds
                yearn for earth.

The soul of dawn
                echoes into dusk
        as crickets sing
to the rising moon
and wild horses gallop
        through the blood
                of twilight.

Father and son
hold fishing poles in stillness
beside their fire
                by the lake,
waiting for dinner.

Balloon riders in the water
reflect the evening sky.

THE VILLAGE OF VIKOS

I watch a shepherd
watching me
as I look to his sheep
and the valley beyond.

What has brought me
to this green place?

How long will it be green?

Only here,
safe from the gray of civilization.

Even green
watching me,

only here.

Emptiness

A madrigal

        in the garden

            for an audience

                of tired insects.

If you are empty,

        you have capacity.

Treetops wave

            as the universe

                whispers to herself.

The smell of rain, cardamom,

            infant grass.

An empty wine glass—

        invisible upon

           a busy table.

Filled with wine,

       the glass is seen.

The universe is empty

       because all is one.

To create is to fill

             the recesses

of your soul.

Once filled,

       you may see

             yourself.

SPEAKING

Clouds melt into dark oak
and rain
fragments silence.

Shadow of laurel branch
speaks to the pavement,
dim in streetlight pale.

Crickets converse
from one side
of the driveway
to the other,
their subtle dialogue
upstaged for a moment
by the girls yelling
in the fourth-story window
across the street.

Dots of rain
upon hedges
will vanish with dawn
as dark oak dissolves
into lenient day.

After the Funeral

I watched the rain
falling into a puddle
for at least an hour tonight.

But it wasn't the rain
or even the puddle,
but the reflection of the streetlight
and the way the rain shattered it
and contorted it into a million
ribbons of white fire,
and how night encased it.

And the light in the puddle
was the only light in the world.

I sat for an hour, listening,
as it sang to me in dark octaves
of sonorous, brilliant flame.

HUNGER

Spider spins

        as day turns youthful.

A late August chill

        foreshadows the fall

        of summer.

Undressing treetops frame

        waning moon.

The web catches nothing—

the moth has already died.

THE BRICK IS REALLY A PIXEL

Blood of the doe,
    white forest floor
spatters.

Falling snow fills
    wolf prints.

Lost amid stars,
tops of telephone poles,
                crosses.

There's a black rectangle
    in the white sky
  where the brick fell.

Wolf prints fill
        falling snow.

Leafless tree
against silver horizon,

      Night

          alive with lightning.

THE STONE CIRCLE

I am the infinite bird
upon the wings
of the sky.

Mist below sea,
above raincloud.

Atop the mountain island,
I know myself
and yet I do not know myself.

Consciousness creates eyes.
Stone causes dreams.
Perception: smoke and glass.

I look that you feel.
I touch that you see.

Mountain becomes a cloud,
a face,
            myself.

The song of the morning lark
is the song of my heart.

TACTILE

Ancient paint
fragments frame,
black knight butterfly bush.

A forgotten vase
                collects
the sorrow of the sky.

I know
what season it is
by looking at
the evening road.

The way the wind
    frolics
        through the trees
tells me
    life is not a dream.

THREE VIOLINS

The mind is different each moment
and yet it recognizes itself.

Sun sets earlier now,
as grass fades to yellow
and birds fail
to greet the dawn.

What is this mind that changes
and yet persists?

Three violins for early autumn,
two for late.
One for winter.
Two and then three again
for spring.
Four for summer.

This universe.
This cosmic memory.

If the tree were not conscious,

why would its leaves be aflame

amid October frost?

This world.

This eternal melody.

The tree,

naked against white.

A single violin.

The tree, green,

birds that greet the dawn.

Again, three violins.

GRENADINE

She tells me
the coffee smells good
and I don't know
if it's her perfume,
a combination of
grapefruit, lavender and vanilla,
or the way she looks
down at the pot,
immersed in long, orange shadows,
the perking and the sound of her voice,
calm, with a smile in it,
but I sit in my car
after leaving, simply remembering her,
perking coffee, aromatic percussion,
the way it played with her voice
and long morning shadows
on the kitchen counter,
alone with my thoughts of her,
looking into my imagining
of her eyes and feeling as though
we were once together long ago,
the way her citrusy, lavender scent
merged with that of the coffee,
in a kitchen now filled
with aromatic apparitions
and slowly diminishing morning shadow
of my longing for her.

CATERPILLAR ART

A tribe of caterpillars
    dines on
        fresh green leaves.

Roots rest
    where sunlight
      does not reach,
  sipping   from the wet ground

      to repair caterpillar art.

ON DYING

Night inhales the violet essence of sleep.

A gnarled and storm-worn birch
   wends diagonally into winter.

The aroma of the violet
     exhaled in
               the cool of night.

A dream of a violet field
          of scent and
not of sight.

Are clouds
     beyond the horizon,
or is fate behind the face
        of the paper doll?

In the form of violet night
sleeps the essence
        of the violet.

       Tea leaves bleed
into pomegranate juice.

ONE

It is dawn
and it is death—
one in the clothes of the other
and the other in the guise of the one.

Wren of reflection,
kitchen light shatters sun.

Dawn pyramided into puzzles.

Separate and together,
sewn with the eyes of infinity.

Dusk puzzle into dawn light.

A pair, of youth and antiquity,
united in a pyramid of oranges
on a blue street corner.

The source of infinite perspectives
is that of only one.

About Avalini

Avalini's endeavors include publishing, web development, art, photography, music and film.

We are located approximately one hour west of Boston, Massachusetts.

Avalini welcomes submissions from new members. For submission guidelines and information about us, visit www.avalini.com.